The Modern Gentleman

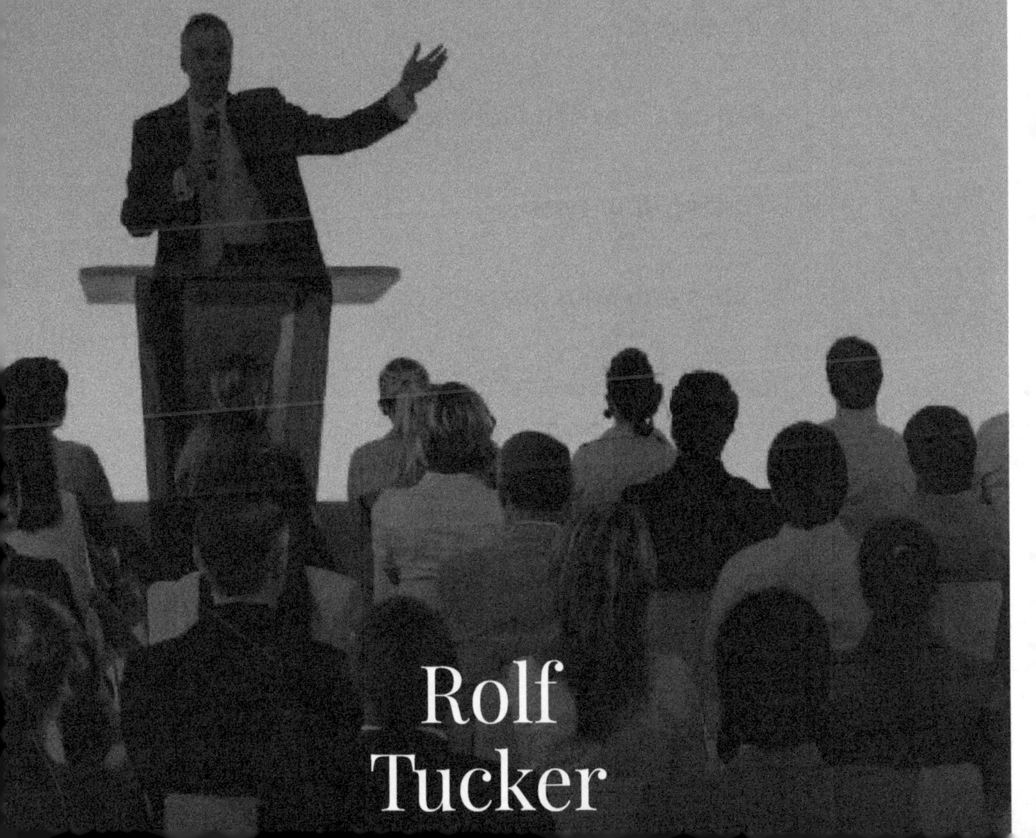

Rolf
Tucker

The Modern Gentleman: A Guide to Dating and Relationships

Table Of Contents

Introduction: Why Being a Modern Gentleman Is Important — 3

Chapter 1: Leveling Up as a Man — 4

    The Importance of Self-Improvement — 4

    Setting Goals and Creating a Plan — 5

    Finding Your Passion — 6

    Cultivating Your Personal Style — 7

Chapter 2: Confidence-Building Techniques for Men — 9

The Modern Gentleman: A Guide to Dating and Relationships

Overcoming Fear and Anxiety	9
Developing a Positive Mindset	10
Improving Body Language	11
Practicing Effective Communication	12
Chapter 3: Dating and Relationship Advice for Men	13
Understanding Women	14
Approaching Women with Confidence	15
Navigating the Early Stages of a Relationship	16
Maintaining a Healthy Relationship	17

# The Modern Gentleman: A Guide to Dating and Relationships

Chapter 4: Mastering the Art of Chivalry	19
The Importance of Respect and Courtesy	19
Being a Good Listener	20
Showing Appreciation and Gratitude	21
Being a Leader and Taking Initiative	22
Chapter 5: Navigating Modern Dating Challenges	23
Dealing with Online Dating	23
Handling Rejection	24
Avoiding Common Dating Mistakes	26

The Modern Gentleman: A Guide to Dating and Relationships

Maintaining Your Independence in a Relationship	27
Conclusion: Becoming the Modern Gentleman You Want to Be.	28

Introduction: Why Being a Modern Gentleman Is Important

Introduction: Why Being a Modern Gentleman Is Important

In today's fast-paced world, being a gentleman may seem outdated. However, it is more important than ever to be a modern gentleman. Being a gentleman is not about being weak or subservient, but about being respectful, courteous, and confident. It is about being the best version of yourself and treating others with kindness and empathy.

Being a modern gentleman is important because it sets you apart from the crowd. It shows that you are not afraid to stand out and be different. Women appreciate a man who is chivalrous and respectful, and being a modern gentleman can help you attract the right kind of person into your life.

The Modern Gentleman: A Guide to Dating and Relationships

Being a modern gentleman is also important because it helps you build confidence. When you treat others with respect and kindness, you feel good about yourself. Confidence is essential in all aspects of life, including dating and relationships. When you are confident, you are more likely to attract the right kind of person into your life.

Being a modern gentleman is not just about how you treat others; it is also about how you treat yourself. A modern gentleman takes care of his appearance and his health. He is aware of his strengths and weaknesses and is always working to improve himself.

In this book, we will explore what it means to be a modern gentleman and how you can become one. We will discuss confidence-building techniques, dating and relationship advice, and how to level up as a man. Whether you are single or in a relationship, this book will provide you with the tools and strategies you need to become the best version of yourself.

The Modern Gentleman: A Guide to Dating and Relationships

Being a modern gentleman is not about being perfect. It is about striving to be the best version of yourself and treating others with kindness and respect. It is about building confidence and attracting positive relationships into your life. So, let's dive in and explore what it means to be a modern gentleman.

Chapter 1: Leveling Up as a Man

The Importance of Self-Improvement

The Importance of Self-Improvement

As a young adult male, it is important to understand the value of self-improvement. The journey of self-improvement is one that never truly ends, as there is always room for growth and development. By actively working on bettering yourself, you can enhance your life in a multitude of ways, including your dating and relationship experiences.

The Modern Gentleman: A Guide to Dating and Relationships

Leveling up as a man requires a commitment to personal growth, which can be achieved through self-improvement. This involves taking control of your life and actively working to become the best version of yourself. This may include developing new skills, pursuing hobbies, practicing good habits, and working on your physical and mental health.

Confidence-building techniques can also be beneficial in the pursuit of self-improvement. Confidence is an attractive trait that can help you in all areas of your life, including dating and relationships. By practicing self-affirmations, setting achievable goals, and stepping outside of your comfort zone, you can increase your confidence and become a more desirable partner.

The Modern Gentleman: A Guide to Dating and Relationships

In addition to improving your personal qualities, self-improvement can also benefit your dating and relationship experiences. By working on yourself, you become more self-aware and better equipped to handle challenges that may arise in your relationships. You can also develop better communication skills, learn to manage conflict, and become more emotionally intelligent.

Ultimately, the importance of self-improvement lies in the fact that it allows you to live a more fulfilling life. By continuously working on yourself, you can achieve your goals, enhance your relationships, and become a more confident and successful individual. So, take the time to invest in yourself and prioritize your personal growth. The benefits will be invaluable.

Setting Goals and Creating a Plan

Setting Goals and Creating a Plan

The Modern Gentleman: A Guide to Dating and Relationships

As a young adult male, it's important to have a goal in mind. Whether it's personal or professional, having a direction in life can help you achieve success and fulfillment. When it comes to dating and relationships, setting goals and creating a plan can be just as important.

The first step in setting goals is to identify what you want to achieve. Do you want to find a long-term partner, or are you just looking for casual dating experiences? Maybe you want to work on improving your communication skills or becoming more confident in yourself. Whatever your goals may be, it's important to be specific and realistic.

Once you have identified your goals, the next step is to create a plan. This can involve a variety of strategies, including improving your social skills, working on your physical appearance, or seeking out new dating opportunities. It's important to break down your goals into smaller, more manageable steps that you can take on a daily basis.

The Modern Gentleman: A Guide to Dating and Relationships

One effective technique for creating a plan is to use the SMART method. This acronym stands for Specific, Measurable, Achievable, Relevant, and Time-bound. By setting specific, measurable goals that are achievable within a certain timeframe, you can track your progress and adjust your plan accordingly.

Another important aspect of setting goals and creating a plan is to stay motivated. This can involve surrounding yourself with positive influences, seeking out support from friends and family, or setting up rewards for yourself as you reach certain milestones. It's important to remember that setbacks and failures are a natural part of the process, and that persistence and perseverance are key to achieving your goals.

Ultimately, setting goals and creating a plan can help you become a more confident, successful, and fulfilled individual in all aspects of your life. By taking small steps towards your goals each day, and staying focused and motivated, you can achieve great things and improve your dating and relationship experiences.

The Modern Gentleman: A Guide to Dating and Relationships

Finding Your Passion

Finding Your Passion

As a young adult male, it's easy to get caught up in the day-to-day grind of work, school, and social obligations. But it's important to remember that life is short, and you only get one shot at it. That's why finding your passion is so crucial.

Your passion is the thing that ignites your soul, the thing you could do for hours on end without getting tired or bored. It's what makes you feel alive and gives your life purpose. And when you're passionate about something, you're more likely to be successful, fulfilled, and happy.

So how do you find your passion? Here are a few tips to get you started:

1. Try new things.

The Modern Gentleman: A Guide to Dating and Relationships

You can't know what you're passionate about until you try new things. So be open to new experiences and try things you've never done before. Take a cooking class, try a new sport, attend a concert, or volunteer for a cause you care about. You never know what might ignite your passion.

2. Pay attention to what excites you.

When you're trying new things, pay attention to what excites you. What makes you feel energized, inspired, and alive? What do you find yourself daydreaming about? These are clues to your passions.

3. Look for patterns.

As you explore different activities and interests, look for patterns. Do you find yourself drawn to anything in particular? Do you have a natural talent or aptitude for something? These are also clues to your passions.

The Modern Gentleman: A Guide to Dating and Relationships

4. Follow your curiosity.

Curiosity is a powerful motivator. If you're curious about something, follow that curiosity. Read books, watch videos, take classes, and talk to people who are experts in that field. You never know where your curiosity might lead you.

Once you've identified your passion, it's important to make time for it in your life. Schedule time to pursue your passion, even if it's just a few hours a week. And don't be afraid to make changes in your life to accommodate your passion. Your passion is what makes life worth living, so don't let it take a backseat to other obligations.

In conclusion, finding your passion is an essential part of level up as a man and building confidence. It can also improve your dating and relationship prospects as it allows you to be more interesting and engaging. Take the time to explore new things, pay attention to what excites you, look for patterns, and follow your curiosity. Your passion is waiting for you.

Cultivating Your Personal Style

Cultivating Your Personal Style

As a modern gentleman, it's important to cultivate your personal style. Your style is a reflection of who you are and how you want to present yourself to the world. Whether you're dressing for a date, a job interview, or just everyday life, your personal style can make a big difference in how people perceive you.

Here are some tips for cultivating your personal style:

The Modern Gentleman: A Guide to Dating and Relationships

1. Know your body type. Understanding your body type is the first step to dressing well. Whether you're tall and thin, short and stocky, or somewhere in between, there are certain styles and cuts that will flatter your body type. Take the time to figure out what works best for you.

2. Invest in quality pieces. It's better to have a few high-quality pieces in your wardrobe than a bunch of cheap, poorly-made clothes. Invest in well-made suits, dress shoes, and other key pieces that will last you for years to come.

3. Mix and match. Don't be afraid to mix and match different pieces to create your own unique look. Experiment with different colors, patterns, and textures to find what works best for you.

4. Pay attention to details. The little things can make a big difference when it comes to style. Pay attention to details like your shoes, accessories, and grooming. A well-groomed beard or a stylish watch can take your look to the next level.

5. Be confident. Ultimately, the key to cultivating your personal style is to be confident in yourself and your choices. Wear what makes you feel good and don't worry too much about what other people think. Your style should be a reflection of who you are, not who you think you should be.

By following these tips, you can cultivate a personal style that reflects your personality and helps you stand out from the crowd. Remember, style is not just about how you look, but how you feel. When you feel good about yourself, it shows in everything you do. So take the time to cultivate your personal style and become the best version of yourself.

Chapter 2: Confidence-Building Techniques for Men

Overcoming Fear and Anxiety

The Modern Gentleman: A Guide to Dating and Relationships

Fear and anxiety are two emotions that can cripple a man's ability to level up in life, build confidence, and succeed in dating and relationships. It is normal to experience fear and anxiety in certain situations, but when these emotions become overwhelming and start to affect your daily life, it's time to take action.

One way to overcome fear and anxiety is to face them head-on. This means exposing yourself to the things that make you anxious or afraid. For example, if you are afraid of public speaking, start by speaking up in small group settings and gradually work your way up to larger audiences. The more you confront your fears, the more comfortable you will become, and the less power they will have over you.

Another technique for overcoming fear and anxiety is mindfulness. Mindfulness is the practice of being aware of the present moment and accepting your thoughts and feelings without judgment. When you are mindful, you can observe your emotions and thoughts without getting caught up in them. This can help you better manage your anxiety and fear.

Physical exercise is also an effective way to manage anxiety and fear. Exercise releases endorphins, which are natural mood-boosters. Regular exercise can help reduce feelings of anxiety and fear and improve your overall mood.

Finally, seeking professional help is always an option. If your fear and anxiety are interfering with your daily life, it may be time to see a therapist or counselor. A mental health professional can help you identify the root causes of your anxiety and develop coping strategies to manage it.

In conclusion, fear and anxiety are common emotions, but they don't have to control your life. By facing your fears, practicing mindfulness, exercising regularly, and seeking professional help when necessary, you can overcome these emotions and become a more confident, successful, and fulfilled modern gentleman.

Developing a Positive Mindset

Developing a Positive Mindset

A positive mindset is one of the most important things a person can cultivate. It can help you see the world in a more optimistic light, and it can lead to better relationships, more success, and greater happiness. Developing a positive mindset takes time and effort, but it is well worth it. Here are some tips to get you started.

1. Focus on the good.

The Modern Gentleman: A Guide to Dating and Relationships

One of the simplest ways to develop a positive mindset is to focus on the good things in your life. Instead of dwelling on the negative, make a conscious effort to recognize the positive. Take a few minutes each day to write down things that you are grateful for. This can help shift your mindset from one of lack to one of abundance.

2. Practice self-care.

Self-care is essential for developing a positive mindset. It involves taking care of your physical, mental, and emotional health. This can include things like exercise, eating well, getting enough sleep, and practicing mindfulness. When you take care of yourself, you are better able to handle the challenges that life throws your way.

3. Surround yourself with positivity.

The Modern Gentleman: A Guide to Dating and Relationships

The people you surround yourself with can have a big impact on your mindset. Seek out friends and mentors who are positive and supportive. Avoid people who are negative or who bring you down. You can also surround yourself with positivity by listening to uplifting music, reading inspiring books, and watching motivational videos.

4. Embrace failure.

Failure is a natural part of life, and it can be a valuable learning experience. Instead of viewing failure as a negative thing, embrace it as an opportunity to grow and learn. When you make a mistake, take the time to reflect on what happened and what you can do differently next time.

5. Practice positive self-talk.

The way you talk to yourself can have a big impact on your mindset. Make a conscious effort to replace negative self-talk with positive affirmations. For example, instead of saying "I can't do this," say "I am capable and confident." This can help boost your self-esteem and lead to a more positive outlook on life.

In conclusion, developing a positive mindset takes time and effort, but it is well worth it. By focusing on the good, practicing self-care, surrounding yourself with positivity, embracing failure, and practicing positive self-talk, you can cultivate a more optimistic and joyful outlook on life.

Improving Body Language

Improving Body Language

The Modern Gentleman: A Guide to Dating and Relationships

Body language is one of the most important aspects of communication. It is often said that actions speak louder than words, and this is especially true when it comes to dating and relationships. Your body language can convey a lot about your personality, your confidence, and your intentions. Therefore, it is essential to learn how to control and improve your body language to improve your chances of success in dating and relationships.

The first step to improving your body language is to become aware of it. Pay attention to how you carry yourself, how you stand, and how you move. Are you slouching? Are you fidgeting? Are you making eye contact? These are all important aspects of body language that can either make or break your chances with the opposite sex. Once you are aware of your body language, you can start working on improving it.

The Modern Gentleman: A Guide to Dating and Relationships

The most important aspect of body language is confidence. If you appear confident, you are more likely to attract others. To improve your confidence, start by standing up straight with your shoulders back. This will give the impression that you are strong and confident. Avoid crossing your arms or legs, as this can make you appear closed off and defensive.

Another important aspect of body language is eye contact. Making eye contact is a sign of confidence and interest. When you are talking to someone, look them in the eye. Avoid looking around the room or checking your phone, as this can give the impression that you are not interested in what they have to say.

Finally, be aware of your gestures. Gestures can be a powerful tool in communication, but they can also be distracting or confusing. Use gestures sparingly and make sure they are appropriate for the situation. Avoid fidgeting or playing with your hair or clothing, as this can be distracting and make you appear nervous or unsure.

Improving your body language is essential if you want to level up as a man. By improving your confidence, making eye contact, and using appropriate gestures, you can improve your chances in dating and relationships. Practice these techniques until they become second nature, and you will be well on your way to becoming a modern gentleman.

Practicing Effective Communication

Effective communication is an essential skill for any man who wants to level up in life and succeed in his dating and relationships. Whether you're trying to impress a potential partner, connect with friends, or advance in your career, the ability to express yourself clearly and effectively is crucial. In this chapter, we'll explore some tips and techniques for practicing effective communication that will help you build confidence, improve your relationships, and achieve your goals.

The Modern Gentleman: A Guide to Dating and Relationships

The first step to practicing effective communication is to be aware of your own thoughts and feelings. Before you can express yourself to others, you need to understand your own emotions and opinions. Take some time each day to reflect on your experiences and try to identify your own thoughts and feelings. This will help you to communicate more authentically and confidently.

Once you're aware of your own thoughts and feelings, it's important to be an active listener. This means paying attention to what others are saying, and responding thoughtfully and empathetically. When you're talking with someone, try to genuinely listen to what they're saying, and demonstrate your understanding by paraphrasing or summarizing their message. This will help to build trust and rapport, and will make others more likely to listen to you in return.

Another key aspect of effective communication is being assertive. This means expressing your own opinions and needs in a clear and direct manner, without being aggressive or confrontational. When you're having a conversation, make sure to speak confidently and avoid apologizing for your opinions or ideas. However, it's also important to be respectful of others' opinions and to avoid dominating the conversation.

Finally, it's important to practice active communication skills in all aspects of your life. Whether you're at work, on a date, or hanging out with friends, try to use these techniques to build stronger relationships and achieve your goals. With practice, you'll become a more effective communicator and a more confident and successful man.

Chapter 3: Dating and Relationship Advice for Men

Understanding Women

The Modern Gentleman: A Guide to Dating and Relationships

Understanding Women

As a young adult male, you may have heard the phrase "women are a mystery" or "women are difficult to understand." While it may seem like an impossible task to fully comprehend the complexities of women, it is important to make an effort to understand them in order to have successful relationships.

First and foremost, it is important to recognize that women are individuals with their own unique thoughts, feelings, and experiences. They should not be treated as a monolithic group with one set of characteristics. However, there are some generalizations that can be made about women that may help you understand them better.

The Modern Gentleman: A Guide to Dating and Relationships

One common trait among women is that they value communication and emotional connection. This means that they often want to talk about their feelings and have their partners listen and respond empathetically. It is important to make an effort to understand and validate their emotions, even if you do not necessarily feel the same way.

Another trait that is often associated with women is that they value security and stability. This may manifest in different ways, such as wanting a stable job or a committed relationship. It is important to show that you are reliable and trustworthy in order to build trust and a sense of security.

Women also tend to be more intuitive and attuned to nonverbal cues than men. This means that they may notice small changes in body language or tone of voice that may indicate something is wrong. It is important to be mindful of your own nonverbal communication and to be aware of how it may be perceived by others.

The Modern Gentleman: A Guide to Dating and Relationships

Overall, understanding women requires a willingness to listen, communicate, and empathize. By recognizing their individuality and being mindful of their values and traits, you can build strong, meaningful relationships with the women in your life.

Approaching Women with Confidence

Approaching Women with Confidence

Approaching women can be a daunting experience for many young adult males. Fear of rejection, feelings of inadequacy, and social anxiety are common emotions that can make it challenging to take the first step in initiating a conversation with a woman. However, with the right mindset and confidence-building techniques, approaching women can become a more comfortable and natural experience.

The Modern Gentleman: A Guide to Dating and Relationships

Firstly, it's essential to understand that rejection is a natural part of the dating process. Not every woman will be interested in you, and that's okay. It's crucial to approach women with the mindset that you have nothing to lose and everything to gain. If you're rejected, it's not a reflection of your worth as a person, but rather an indication that you and that particular woman weren't a match.

One of the keys to approaching women with confidence is to believe in yourself. Self-confidence is a powerful tool that can help you overcome fears and insecurities. Take the time to develop a positive self-image by focusing on your strengths, accomplishments, and unique qualities. When you feel good about yourself, it's easier to approach women with confidence and ease.

The Modern Gentleman: A Guide to Dating and Relationships

Another technique to build confidence when approaching women is to practice. The more you put yourself out there and initiate conversations with women, the more comfortable and confident you'll become. Start by approaching women in low-pressure situations, such as at a coffee shop or bookstore. Gradually work your way up to more challenging situations, such as approaching a woman at a bar or club.

When approaching women, it's essential to be genuine and authentic. Women can sense when someone is being insincere or trying too hard. Instead, focus on being yourself and showing interest in the woman you're approaching. Ask open-ended questions and actively listen to her responses. Take the time to get to know her, and you'll increase your chances of building a connection.

In conclusion, approaching women with confidence is an essential aspect of dating and relationships. By developing a positive mindset, practicing, and being genuine, you'll increase your chances of success. Remember, rejection is a natural part of the dating process, and it's essential to approach each situation with an open mind and a willingness to learn. With these techniques, you'll become a more confident and successful dater.

Navigating the Early Stages of a Relationship

Navigating the Early Stages of a Relationship

Starting a new relationship can be both exciting and nerve-wracking at the same time. You may have met someone you really like, but you're not sure how to make things work. The early stages of a relationship can be tricky, but with the right mindset and approach, you can navigate them successfully. Here are some tips to help you get started.

The Modern Gentleman: A Guide to Dating and Relationships

Be Honest with Yourself

Before you can be honest with anyone else, you need to be honest with yourself. Take some time to reflect on what you want from a relationship and what you're looking for in a partner. Are you ready for a serious commitment, or are you just looking to have fun? Be honest with yourself about your intentions and make sure you communicate them clearly to your partner.

Take Things Slow

There's no need to rush into anything when you're starting a new relationship. Take things slow and enjoy the process. Get to know your partner and let them get to know you. Don't put too much pressure on yourself or your partner to make things work right away. Give yourselves time to see if you're a good match for each other.

Communicate Clearly

The Modern Gentleman: A Guide to Dating and Relationships

Communication is key in any relationship, especially in the early stages. Be open and honest with your partner about your feelings, thoughts, and expectations. Don't be afraid to ask questions and listen to their answers. If something is bothering you, speak up and address it calmly and respectfully. Avoid playing games or being passive-aggressive.

Be Yourself

One of the most important things you can do in a new relationship is to be yourself. Don't try to be someone you're not or pretend to like things you don't. Your partner should like you for who you are, not for who you're trying to be. Be confident in yourself and your abilities, and don't be afraid to show your true colors.

In conclusion, the early stages of a relationship can be both exciting and challenging. With the right mindset and approach, you can navigate them successfully. Be honest with yourself and your partner, take things slow, communicate clearly, and be yourself. Remember, a healthy and fulfilling relationship takes time and effort from both partners. Good luck!

Maintaining a Healthy Relationship

Maintaining a Healthy Relationship

Congratulations! You have found someone you want to be in a relationship with. Now, the question is, how do you maintain a healthy relationship? Relationships are like a plant; you need to water them regularly, give them proper care and attention, and provide them with the right environment to grow.

Here are some tips on how to maintain a healthy relationship:

1. Communication is key

The Modern Gentleman: A Guide to Dating and Relationships

Communication is the foundation of any healthy relationship. It's essential to communicate your feelings, thoughts, and concerns openly and honestly with your partner. Listen to what they have to say and try to understand their perspective. Don't interrupt, and don't judge them. Remember, it's not about who is right or wrong; it's about finding a solution that works for both of you.

2. Respect each other

Respect is a crucial element in any relationship. Respect your partner's thoughts, feelings, and boundaries. Don't belittle or criticize them. Instead, try to understand them and their point of view. Be sensitive to their needs and feelings, and don't dismiss them.

3. Be supportive

The Modern Gentleman: A Guide to Dating and Relationships

Supporting your partner is essential in a healthy relationship. Be their cheerleader, encourage them, and help them achieve their goals. Be there for them when they need you, and celebrate their successes together.

4. Keep the romance alive

It's easy to get caught up in the daily routine and forget to show affection towards your partner. Make an effort to keep the romance alive by doing small things that show you care. Surprise them with a thoughtful gesture, plan a date night, or leave them a love note. These small gestures can go a long way in keeping the spark alive.

5. Work through conflicts

No relationship is perfect, and conflicts will arise. It's important to work through these conflicts together, rather than avoiding them or sweeping them under the rug. Address the issue, listen to each other's perspectives, and find a solution that works for both of you.

In conclusion, maintaining a healthy relationship is not rocket science. It requires effort, commitment, and a willingness to work through the ups and downs. Remember to communicate openly and honestly, respect each other, be supportive, keep the romance alive, and work through conflicts. By following these tips, you'll be well on your way to building a strong and healthy relationship.

Chapter 4: Mastering the Art of Chivalry

The Importance of Respect and Courtesy

The Modern Gentleman: A Guide to Dating and Relationships

Respect and courtesy are fundamental values that every modern gentleman should possess. They form the basis of every healthy relationship, whether it is a romantic one or a platonic one. As a young adult male, you must understand the importance of treating others with respect and courtesy, as it can help you build stronger and more meaningful relationships with people.

Respect and courtesy are essential in building a positive reputation. When you treat people with respect and courtesy, you demonstrate that you are a gentleman who values others' feelings and opinions. This creates a positive image of you in the minds of others, and people are more likely to want to associate with you.

The Modern Gentleman: A Guide to Dating and Relationships

In romantic relationships, respect and courtesy are crucial. It is essential to treat your partner with respect, even in moments of disagreement or conflict. This means listening to their concerns and opinions without dismissing them, and communicating with them in a respectful and non-condescending manner. Courtesy also plays a significant role in romantic relationships. Small gestures like opening doors, pulling out chairs, and giving compliments can make a big difference in how your partner perceives you.

Respect and courtesy are also important in building confidence. When you treat others with respect and courtesy, you demonstrate that you are confident in yourself and your abilities. This can help you feel more confident in social situations and make it easier to connect with people.

In conclusion, respect and courtesy are essential values that every modern gentleman should possess. They form the foundation of healthy relationships and help build a positive reputation. By treating others with respect and courtesy, you demonstrate confidence in yourself and your abilities. As a young adult male, it is essential to understand the importance of these values and incorporate them into your daily life.

Being a Good Listener

Being a Good Listener

One of the most important skills you can develop as a modern gentleman is the ability to be a good listener. In today's fast-paced world, people often feel unheard and undervalued. By being a good listener, you can set yourself apart and forge deeper, more meaningful connections with those around you.

Here are some tips on how to be a good listener:

The Modern Gentleman: A Guide to Dating and Relationships

1. Pay Attention

The first step in being a good listener is to pay attention. When someone is speaking to you, put down your phone, turn off the TV, and give them your full attention. Make eye contact and nod your head to show that you are listening.

2. Don't Interrupt

Interrupting someone while they are speaking is a surefire way to make them feel unheard and undervalued. Wait until they have finished speaking before responding. If you need clarification, ask questions to show that you are interested in what they have to say.

3. Show Empathy

The Modern Gentleman: A Guide to Dating and Relationships

Empathy is the ability to understand and share the feelings of another person. When someone is speaking to you, try to put yourself in their shoes and imagine how they are feeling. This will help you to respond in a way that is empathetic and supportive.

4. Avoid Judgement

When someone is sharing their thoughts and feelings with you, it is important to avoid judgement. Even if you don't agree with what they are saying, try to understand their perspective and respond in a way that is respectful and non-judgmental.

5. Reflect Back

One technique that can help you to be a better listener is to reflect back what the other person is saying. This means paraphrasing what they have said in your own words. It shows that you are listening and can help to clarify any misunderstandings.

By being a good listener, you can build stronger relationships with those around you and become a more empathetic and understanding person. Practice these tips and make a conscious effort to listen more and talk less. Your relationships will thank you for it.

Showing Appreciation and Gratitude

Showing Appreciation and Gratitude

One of the most important traits of a modern gentleman is the ability to express appreciation and gratitude. Whether it's to a friend, family member, or romantic partner, showing gratitude is a sign of respect and a way to strengthen relationships. In this chapter, we'll explore some simple ways to demonstrate appreciation and gratitude in your daily life.

The Modern Gentleman: A Guide to Dating and Relationships

First off, it's important to recognize the value of saying "thank you." This simple phrase can go a long way in showing someone that you appreciate their efforts. Whether it's a colleague who helped you with a project or a partner who cooked you dinner, taking the time to say "thank you" shows that you don't take their kindness for granted.

Another way to show appreciation is through small gestures. This could be as simple as bringing a friend their favorite coffee or surprising your partner with a thoughtful gift. These small acts of kindness show that you are paying attention to their needs and that you care about their happiness.

The Modern Gentleman: A Guide to Dating and Relationships

In addition to showing appreciation, expressing gratitude is also important. This means taking the time to reflect on all the good things in your life and acknowledging the people who have helped you along the way. Whether it's your parents who supported you through college or a mentor who gave you career advice, expressing gratitude can help strengthen these relationships and build a sense of community.

Finally, it's important to remember that showing appreciation and gratitude isn't just about others. It's also about recognizing your own accomplishments and giving yourself credit where credit is due. This means taking the time to acknowledge your own hard work and celebrating your successes.

In conclusion, showing appreciation and gratitude is an important trait of a modern gentleman. By taking the time to say "thank you," performing small acts of kindness, expressing gratitude, and acknowledging your own accomplishments, you can build stronger relationships and a more positive outlook on life.

Being a Leader and Taking Initiative

Being a Leader and Taking Initiative

Leadership is not the exclusive domain of CEOs, politicians or generals. It is a quality that every man should aspire to possess. Being a leader means taking charge of your life, making decisions that shape your destiny, and inspiring others to follow your example. It is a quality that is highly valued in the workplace, in social situations, and in romantic relationships.

If you want to level up as a man, you need to develop your leadership skills. This means taking initiative, being proactive, and taking responsibility for your actions. It means having the courage to take risks, to step out of your comfort zone, and to embrace new challenges. It also means being willing to learn from your mistakes, to adapt to changing circumstances, and to keep moving forward.

The Modern Gentleman: A Guide to Dating and Relationships

Confidence is a key component of leadership, and it is something that can be developed through practice and experience. Confidence-building techniques for men include setting goals, visualizing success, and taking action. When you set goals, you give yourself a clear direction and a sense of purpose. When you visualize success, you create a mental picture of what you want to achieve, and you focus your energy and attention on that goal. When you take action, you build momentum and create opportunities for success.

In dating and relationships, being a leader means taking the initiative to ask someone out, to plan a date, or to make a romantic gesture. It means being confident in yourself and your abilities, and being willing to take the lead when necessary. It also means being a good listener, being empathetic, and being supportive of your partner's goals and aspirations.

Being a leader is not about being dominant or controlling. It is about being responsible, respectful, and inspiring. It is about being the best version of yourself, and helping others to do the same. If you want to be a modern gentleman, you need to embrace the qualities of leadership, and use them to create a life that is rich, fulfilling, and meaningful.

Chapter 5: Navigating Modern Dating Challenges

Dealing with Online Dating

Dealing with Online Dating

In this day and age, it's rare to find someone who hasn't at least tried online dating. It's a convenient way to meet new people, but it can also be overwhelming and frustrating at times. Here are some tips for dealing with online dating:

The Modern Gentleman: A Guide to Dating and Relationships

1. Be honest with yourself. Before you even start swiping, take a moment to think about what you're looking for. Are you just looking for a casual hookup, or are you looking for something more serious? Be honest with yourself about your intentions so that you can find someone who is on the same page as you.

2. Don't take it too seriously. It's important to remember that online dating is just one way to meet people. Don't put too much pressure on yourself or the people you're talking to. Enjoy the process and have fun with it.

3. Be selective. It's easy to get caught up in the endless options of online dating, but remember that quality is better than quantity. Take the time to read someone's profile and decide if they're someone you're genuinely interested in before swiping right.

4. Use good photos. Your photos are the first thing people will see when they come across your profile, so make sure they're good. Use clear, well-lit photos that show your face and personality.

5. Be respectful. Just because you're behind a screen doesn't mean you should treat people any differently than you would in person. Be respectful and kind, even if you're not interested in someone.

6. Don't give up. Online dating can be discouraging at times, but don't give up. Keep putting yourself out there and eventually you'll find someone who is a good match for you.

Remember, online dating is just one option for meeting people. Don't rely solely on it and don't let it consume your life. Stay true to yourself and have fun with it.

Handling Rejection

Handling Rejection

The Modern Gentleman: A Guide to Dating and Relationships

Rejection is an inevitable part of life, especially when it comes to dating and relationships. But just because it's inevitable doesn't mean that it's easy to handle. Rejection can be painful, frustrating, and can shake your confidence. However, it's important to remember that rejection is not a reflection of your worth as a person. It's simply a sign that the person you're interested in is not interested in you in the same way. Here are some tips for handling rejection like a gentleman:

1. Don't take it personally

As mentioned earlier, rejection is not a reflection of your worth as a person. It's important to remember that the person who rejected you is not rejecting you as a person, but rather the idea of being in a romantic relationship with you. Don't take it personally and don't let it affect your self-esteem.

2. Take time to process your emotions

The Modern Gentleman: A Guide to Dating and Relationships

It's okay to feel sad, disappointed, or frustrated after being rejected. Take some time to process your emotions and allow yourself to feel them. Don't suppress your emotions or pretend that you're okay when you're not. It's important to acknowledge your emotions so that you can start to move on.

3. Learn from the experience

Rejection can also be a learning experience. Think about what went wrong and what you could have done differently. Were there any red flags that you ignored? Did you come on too strong? Use this experience as an opportunity to grow and improve yourself.

4. Keep your chin up

The Modern Gentleman: A Guide to Dating and Relationships

After being rejected, it's easy to feel discouraged and lose confidence. However, it's important to keep your chin up and not let rejection define you. Remember that there are plenty of other people out there who would be interested in dating you. Keep putting yourself out there and don't give up.

In conclusion, handling rejection is never easy, but it's an important part of dating and relationships. Remember to not take it personally, take time to process your emotions, learn from the experience, and keep your chin up. By handling rejection like a gentleman, you'll be able to build your confidence and level up as a man in all aspects of your life.

Avoiding Common Dating Mistakes

Avoiding Common Dating Mistakes

The Modern Gentleman: A Guide to Dating and Relationships

As a young adult male, dating and relationships can be a daunting and confusing experience. However, there are some common mistakes that you can avoid to increase your chances of success. Here are some tips to help you navigate the dating world.

1. Don't be too eager

One of the biggest mistakes that men make when dating is being too eager. It's important to show interest and enthusiasm, but you don't want to come across as desperate or needy. Take your time getting to know someone and don't rush into a relationship.

2. Don't be afraid to be yourself

The Modern Gentleman: A Guide to Dating and Relationships

Another common mistake that men make is trying to be someone they're not. It's important to be authentic and true to yourself. Don't pretend to be interested in something just because you think it will impress someone. Be honest about your interests and values, and you'll attract someone who appreciates you for who you are.

3. Don't ignore red flags

When you're dating, it's important to pay attention to red flags. If someone is consistently canceling plans, not responding to your messages, or treating you poorly, it's a sign that they're not interested or not ready for a relationship. Don't ignore these warning signs and continue to pursue someone who isn't interested.

4. Don't neglect self-care

The Modern Gentleman: A Guide to Dating and Relationships

Taking care of yourself is important in all aspects of life, including dating. Make sure you're taking care of your physical and mental health. Exercise regularly, eat a healthy diet, and make time for hobbies and activities that bring you joy. When you feel good about yourself, it will show in your interactions with others.

5. Don't rush into physical intimacy

While physical intimacy is an important part of a relationship, it's important not to rush into it. Take your time getting to know someone and building trust before becoming intimate. Rushing into physical intimacy can lead to misunderstandings and hurt feelings.

By avoiding these common dating mistakes, you'll increase your chances of success in the dating world. Remember to be yourself, pay attention to red flags, take care of yourself, and take your time getting to know someone. Good luck!

Maintaining Your Independence in a Relationship

Maintaining Your Independence in a Relationship

As a young adult male, it's important to understand that maintaining your independence in a relationship is crucial to your overall happiness and success. While being in a relationship can be a wonderful and fulfilling experience, it's important to remember that you are still your own person with your own goals, dreams, and aspirations.

Here are some tips on how to maintain your independence in a relationship:

The Modern Gentleman: A Guide to Dating and Relationships

1. Set boundaries: It's important to set boundaries early on in a relationship. This means being clear about what you're comfortable with and what you're not. This can include things like how much time you need to yourself, how often you want to see your partner, and what activities you want to do together.

2. Pursue your own interests: Don't forget about the things that make you happy outside of your relationship. Whether it's a hobby, a passion project, or just spending time with friends, make sure you're still making time for the things that matter to you.

3. Communicate openly: Communication is key in any relationship, and it's especially important when it comes to maintaining your independence. Be honest with your partner about your needs and feelings, and encourage them to do the same.

The Modern Gentleman: A Guide to Dating and Relationships

4. Don't lose sight of your goals: It's easy to get caught up in a relationship and forget about your own goals and ambitions. Make sure you're still working towards the things you want in life, whether that's a career goal or a personal accomplishment.

5. Remember that it's okay to be alone: Being in a relationship doesn't mean you have to give up your independence entirely. It's okay to spend time alone and enjoy your own company. In fact, it's important to have a healthy relationship with yourself before you can have a healthy relationship with someone else.

By following these tips, you can maintain your independence while still enjoying the benefits of being in a relationship. Remember that a healthy relationship is one where both partners are able to grow and thrive together, while still maintaining their own individuality.

Conclusion: Becoming the Modern Gentleman You Want to Be.

Conclusion: Becoming the Modern Gentleman You Want to Be

Congratulations! By reading this book, you have taken a step towards becoming the modern gentleman you want to be. You have learned about the importance of self-improvement, confidence-building techniques, and dating and relationship advice. Now, it's time to put what you've learned into action.

Becoming a modern gentleman is not an overnight process. It takes time, effort, and dedication. But remember, every step you take towards self-improvement is a step towards becoming the best version of yourself.

The Modern Gentleman: A Guide to Dating and Relationships

One of the most important things you can do to become a modern gentleman is to focus on your personal development. This means taking care of yourself physically, mentally, and emotionally. Get regular exercise, eat a healthy diet, and make time for self-care activities like meditation or hobbies you enjoy. When you take care of yourself, you will feel better and more confident in all areas of your life.

Another important aspect of becoming a modern gentleman is building your confidence. Confidence is key when it comes to dating and relationships. To build your confidence, practice positive self-talk, set and achieve goals, and surround yourself with supportive people who lift you up.

When it comes to dating and relationships, remember that communication is key. Be honest and open with your partner, and listen to their needs and wants. Remember that relationships take work and require compromise. Be willing to put in the time and effort to make your relationship a success.

The Modern Gentleman: A Guide to Dating and Relationships

In conclusion, becoming a modern gentleman is about self-improvement, confidence-building, and developing healthy relationships. Remember that it's a journey, not a destination. Keep working on yourself, and you will become the modern gentleman you want to be. Good luck!

The Modern Gentleman: A Guide to Dating and Relationships

Rolf Tucker

www.ingramcontent.com/pod-product-compliance
Lightning Source LLC
Chambersburg PA
CBHW050446010526
44118CB00013B/1708